NEW LANGUAGE, NEW FRIENDS

By Don Aker

CELEBRATION PRESS
Pearson Learning Group

Contents

Language Opens Doors

There are more than 6,000 languages spoken in the world. How many languages do you speak? If you speak one language, you will only be able to talk with people who speak that same language.

Learning a second or third language will help you to make friends with more people. Someday you may want to visit or live in a place where people speak another language. Learning other languages can open doors to many new opportunities.

There are many ways of saying "hello."

Make Friends

You have probably heard people speaking a language other than your own. It may have been at school, in a store, or in the street. Maybe your parents or grandparents speak another language. You may know people who are from other countries. Many **immigrants** move to a country where people use a different language than the one they speak.

The Five Most-Spoken First Languages

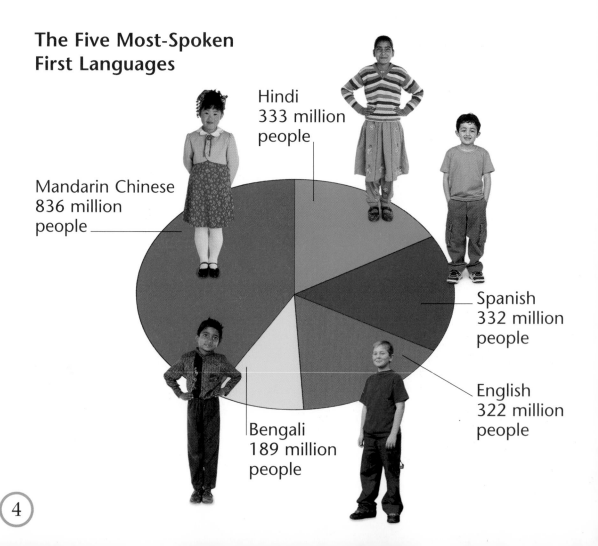

Hindi
333 million
people

Mandarin Chinese
836 million
people

Spanish
332 million
people

English
322 million
people

Bengali
189 million
people

A child from another country might move to yours and not speak your language. You might move to a country where you do not speak the language. Both you and the other child would need to learn a new language.

Try making friends with a child who speaks another language. Ask your friend to teach you a few words. You might learn how to tell a story or a joke. You can also teach your friend words in your language. Sharing words can help you and your friend work and play together. Your lives will become more interesting as you get to know one another.

a drawing

le dessin

You can make friends with children who live in other countries. The children on these pages are from many different countries. Some of these children may look, dress, or act differently from you and your friends, but you might be surprised at how much you have in common. Which of these children share some of your interests?

Canada

NORTH AMERICA

ATLANTIC OCEAN

PACIFIC OCEAN

SOUTH AMERICA

Argentina

Levi (LEE-vi)
Country: Canada
Languages: Inuktitut and English
Likes: toy cars, ice hockey, math, computers

Carlitos (car-LEE-tos)
Country: Argentina
Language: Spanish
Likes: horseback riding, cycling, fishing, playing with his model racing car

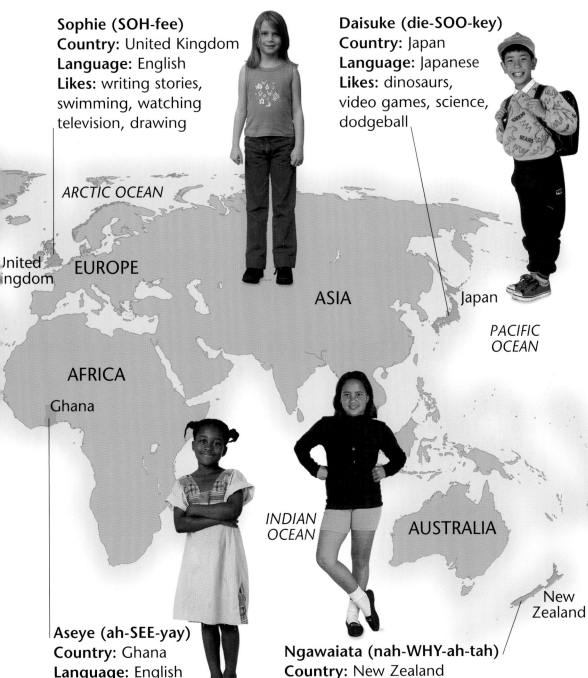

Sophie (SOH-fee)
Country: United Kingdom
Language: English
Likes: writing stories,
swimming, watching
television, drawing

Daisuke (die-SOO-key)
Country: Japan
Language: Japanese
Likes: dinosaurs,
video games, science,
dodgeball

ARCTIC OCEAN

United
Kingdom

EUROPE

ASIA

Japan

*PACIFIC
OCEAN*

AFRICA

Ghana

*INDIAN
OCEAN*

AUSTRALIA

New
Zealand

Aseye (ah-SEE-yay)
Country: Ghana
Language: English
Likes: Drawing,
writing, watching
films, playing games

Ngawaiata (nah-WHY-ah-tah)
Country: New Zealand
Languages: Maori and English
Likes: Swimming, climbing trees,
reading, learning Maori and English

You do not need to travel to make friends in other countries. If you learn another language, you can write to other children all around the world. What would you like to know about them?

Ask your teacher to help you find a pen pal in another country. Writing letters to a friend is a great way to practice a new language. E-mail makes it even easier to stay in touch with friends from around the world.

Try writing new phrases in e-mails. If your pen pal is online at the same time, you might get a fast reply.

Some schools and towns have special programs to connect people around the world. These programs are called sister cities, sister schools, or twin towns. They often have special sites on the Internet where people can e-mail each other. Maybe your city or town has a sister city on the other side of the world. You could ask an adult help you use the Internet to find out more.

Useful Expressions

How do you say "How are you?"

Language	Expression	Pronunciation
Spanish	*Como estás?*	COH-moh es-TAHS
Italian	*Come sta?*	COH-may stah
French	*Comment ça va?*	cuh-MAHN sah vah
Japanese	お元気ですか	oh-hen-kee des-kah

Learn About the World

Learning another language can help you explore a different **culture**. Your own neighborhood could be a good place to start. A place near your home might serve food from other countries. You might learn some words just by reading the menu. Knowing some of these words might help you choose new foods to eat.

roast beef
English meat dish

aloo baigan (AH-loo BAY-gehn)
Indian curry dish

paella (pah-AY-yah)
Spanish rice dish

寿司 (SOO-shee)
Japanese rice and seafood dish

Try ordering your food in another language. Waiters might be able to help you. Ask them to tell you the names of the dishes in that language. Do not worry about making mistakes. People will be happy that you are trying to speak their language.

French menu

You can learn many new food words by reading a menu.

You can also learn about different cultures by visiting a library or a bookstore. Look for books and magazines in other languages. Choose a book about something that interests you in another part of the world. If you know a little of the language, you can read some of the book. You can also learn new words by using the pictures to guide you.

Flip through a book in another language to learn new words.

English

French

Japanese

German

Try watching television shows and movies from other countries. You can also listen to music in another language. These will teach you about other cultures and help you learn new words.

Many libraries have videotapes or DVDs of movies from other countries. They may also have CDs or audiotapes that teach different languages. You can borrow these at some libraries.

Listening to tapes or CDs can help you learn how to pronounce, or say, new words.

Did You Know?

Learning a new language might be easier than you think. There are words in other languages that are similar to English. That's because many languages spoken today come from Latin. Here is an example.

Language	Word	Pronunciation
Latin	*theatrum*	teh-AH-troom
English	*theater*	THEE-uh-ter
Spanish	*teatro*	tay-AH-troh
French	*théâtre*	tay-AH-treh

Someday you may wish to travel to another country. You may see things that you cannot see at home. The buildings, music, food, transportation, and people will be new to you. Traveling is more fun when you can speak some of the language. Then you and your family can talk to people.

This family from India is sight-seeing in London, England.

Language Tip

Take a **phrase book** with you when you travel to another country. A phrase book will teach you how to say useful words and phrases in that language. Learning to say "I would like..." and "Where is...?" can be helpful.

Useful Expressions

How do you say "Thank you"?

Language	Expression	Pronunciation
Spanish	*Gracias*	GRAH-see-ahs
Italian	*Grazie*	GRAH-tsee-ay
French	*Merci*	mehr-SEE
Japanese	どうもありがとう	ah-ree-gah-toh

Your trip to another country may be more interesting if you become friends with people who live there. Speaking the **local** language could help you meet people. You might learn about their lives. They could tell you about themselves and about things they like to do. They could also tell you about some of the best places to visit.

Talk to other children in their language and you might learn new games.

Traveling is also easier when you know some of the language. You will be able to understand the words on signs which might keep you and your family from getting lost. The signs might also lead you to more interesting places. If you learn the words for "beach" and "amusement park," then you could add to your list of places to visit.

underground walkway in Turkey

post office in the Czech Republic

national park in Australia

fish restaurant in Spain

beach in Canada

Knowing the language can help you if there is a problem. For example, you and your family might get lost. Then you would need to ask for directions. The local people may not speak your language. Knowing even a few words in their language can help you. Then you could ask a police officer or a shopkeeper for help.

Useful Expressions

How do you say "Where is ...?"

Language	Expression	Pronunciation
Spanish	*¿Dónde está ...?*	DOHN-day eh-STAH
Italian	*Dove' è ...?*	DOH-vay ay
French	*Où est ...?*	oo ay
Japanese	どこ？	doh-ko dess-ka

Discover Opportunities

Today it is easy to **communicate** with people from many countries. We have e-mail, telephones, text messaging, and fax machines. Transportation is faster and cheaper than it used to be. People from different countries may work, study, and live side by side. That's why it is now so important to learn another language.

Look at a globe. Where would you like to go someday?

Exchange programs help young people learn a language and make friendships.

Someday you may wish to live in another country. When you are a little older, you could take part in an **exchange program**. Young people live with a family in another country for a short time or a school year. They spend time with the family, make friends, and go to school. It is an exciting way to learn about a new country. To do this, you will need to learn the language.

Did You Know?

Your family can **host** an exchange student from another country. The student would live with your family while going to school. Families hosting an exchange student often learn about a new language and culture.

teacher

Many people need to know another language to do their jobs.

Today people often work with others in different countries all over the world. Many companies **employ** people who are able to speak more than one language. It may be easier for you to work someday if you do speak more than one language. You might do business with people in other countries on the phone and through e-mail. You might go to another country to work.

translator

airline pilots

Working Around the World

Speaking another language can be helpful for many jobs such as the ones below.

• **Interpreters/Translators** Interpreters and translators listen to one person speak his or her own language. Then they translate those words into a language that others will understand.

• **Chefs** Restaurants serving food from different countries often need chefs who speak several languages.

• **Reporters** Reporters sometimes travel to other countries to write their articles. They will find more information when they can speak to people in their language.

• **Business people** Some businesses are **international** and have offices in many countries. People who work in them sometimes live in countries other than their own.

• **Teachers** Teachers can work in different countries.

• **Airline crew** Pilots and flight attendants take care of passengers in many different countries.

• **Doctors and Nurses** Doctors and nurses work in many different countries.

Learning another language could make your life interesting in many ways. You could make new friends and traveling and learning about other countries would be easier and more interesting. Knowing more than one language may help you find an exciting job when you are older. Which new language would you like to learn first?

Language Survey

A survey is a way of collecting information about people. Use this survey to find out what languages your classmates speak. Then make a chart that lists those languages, and how many people in your class speak each one.

Language Survey

1. How many languages do you speak?_____

2. What languages do you speak?_____

3. What language do you speak at home?____

4. How many different languages are spoken in your class?_____

Glossary

communicate to share ideas or information with someone

culture the art, beliefs, and traditions of a group of people

employ to hire and pay for work

exchange program a program through which students go to school and live in another country

host to have guests in the home

immigrants people who move to another country

international including people from more than one country

local part of or near an area such as a town or neighborhood

phrase book a small book of helpful words and phrases in another language

translate to repeat information in a different language so others will understand it

Index

Useful Expressions

How do you say "Goodbye"?

Language	Expression	Pronunciation
Spanish	*Adiós*	ah-dee-OHS
Italian	*Arrivederci*	ah-REE-vuh-DAIR-chee
French	*Au revoir*	oh ruh-VWAH
Japanese	さよなら	syh-oh-nah-rah